ECOSYSTEMS
IN ACTION

LIFE IN A DESERT

LIFE IN A DESERT

BY DOROTHY HINSHAW PATENT
PHOTOGRAPHS BY WILLIAM MUÑOZ

Lerner Publications Company
Minneapolis

In memory of John (Jack) Muñoz, who shared his love of the Sonoran Desert with me —D. H. P.

In memory of my father, thank you for your loving encouragement of me —W. A. M.

The author and photographer would like to thank the staff of the Sonoran Desert Museum and the Bryce Arboretum for their help with this book. We'd also like to thank Peter Lesica for his assistance in identifying plant photos.

Text copyright © 2003 by Dorothy Hinshaw Patent

Photographs copyright © 2003 by William Muñoz, except where noted.

Lerner Publications Company
A division of Lerner Publishing Group
241 First Avenue North
Minneapolis, MN 55401 U.S.A.

Website address: www.lernerbooks.com

Library of Congress Cataloging-in-Publication Data

Patent, Dorothy Hinshaw.
    Life in a desert / by Dorothy Hinshaw Patent ; photographs by William Muñoz.
        p.   cm. — (Ecosystems in Action)
    Summary: Examines the physical features, processes, and many different species of plants and animals that make up the ecosystem of the North American Sonoran Desert.
    ISBN: 0–8225–2140–7 (lib. bdg. : alk. paper)
    1. Desert ecology—Sonoran Desert—Juvenile literature. 2. Sonoran Desert—Juvenile literature. [1. Desert ecology. 2. Ecology. 3. Sonoran Desert.] I. Muñoz, William, ill. II. Title. III. Series.
    QH104.5.S58 P38 2003
    577.54'0979—dc21   2002009856

Manufactured in the United States of America
1 2 3 4 5 6 – JR – 08 07 06 05 04 03

CONTENTS

INTRODUCTION
WHAT IS AN ECOSYSTEM?

An ecosystem is a particular community of living things interacting with each other and their nonliving environment. Thus, just about everything is involved in an ecosystem—the weather, the soil, the air, the plants, the animals, and all the other living things, such as bacteria and fungi, that live in it.

A desert ecosystem, such as the Sonoran Desert, is very different from other kinds of ecosystems, such as an old growth forest or a tallgrass prairie. While there may be areas where two ecosystems intermingle along their edges, they are easy to recognize. Forested mountains border the Sonoran Desert on the east and west. Those areas lack the tall cacti such as the saguaro that are typical of the Sonoran Desert. They have trees such as oaks or pines that don't grow in the desert. To the northwest, the Sonoran Desert blends into the Mojave Desert. Both deserts are hot, dry places, but the cooler Mojave gets rain only in the winter, while the Sonoran also gets some rain in the summer. The amount of rainfall is very important in making an ecosystem what it is. Rainfall in the Sonoran Desert is

THE SONORAN DESERT MAY BE A HARSH ENVIRONMENT, BUT IT IS ALSO VERY BEAUTIFUL.

greater than in the Mojave Desert. But the Sonoran Desert has less rain than an oak-and-pine forest.

Partly because of these differences in climate, different plants and animals inhabit the two neighboring desert ecosystems. The giant saguaro cacti of the Sonoran Desert don't live in the Mojave, and the Joshua trees of the Mojave are absent in the Sonoran Desert.

A plant or animal may be restricted to one or two ecosystems. For example, Brewer's sparrow lives in the Mojave Desert but not in the Sonoran Desert. The desert pupfish and the coati, a ring-tailed relative of the raccoon, are found in the Sonoran Desert but not in the Mojave. Other animals, such as the American kestrel, are much more widely adapted and can be found in all the ecosystems in the United States and in much of Canada.

> **THE AMOUNT OF RAINFALL IS VERY IMPORTANT IN MAKING AN ECOSYSTEM WHAT IT IS. RAINFALL IN THE SONORAN DESERT IS GREATER THAN IN THE MOJAVE DESERT. BUT THE SONORAN DESERT HAS LESS RAIN THAN AN OAK-AND-PINE FOREST.**

HOW AN ECOSYSTEM WORKS

Energy and materials flow through an ecosystem. Chemicals, such as water, nitrogen, and carbon, move from one part of an ecosystem to another. Most importantly, the energy of the sun, which reaches the earth as sunshine, is transferred through the ecosystem. The chemical reactions of life, called metabolism, require the input of energy. Without plants to capture the sun's energy, almost all the earth's ecosystems would run out of energy and die.

The sun's energy is stored in the leaves, stems, roots, and flowers of plants. As a plant takes in the energy of the sun, it grows. Plants are called primary producers since they capture the sun's energy and turn it into living material.

Next, a grazing animal such as a Mormon cricket eats the plant. The cricket and other animals that eat plants are called primary consumers. Some of the sun's energy captured by the plant has been converted into the body of the cricket. A snake eats the cricket and is in turn captured by a hawk. Some of the chemicals and energy of the Mormon cricket are transferred first to the snake, then to the hawk. Both the snake and hawk, which eat other animals, are called secondary consumers.

When the hawk dies, its body is consumed by worms, maggots, fungi, and bacteria. The worms, maggots, fungi, and bacteria, which break down dead matter, are called decomposers. What is left returns to the soil to nourish new plants. This constant recycling of energy and chemicals helps keep the ecosystem running smoothly.

The input and output of an ecosystem refer to the things that enter and leave the ecosystem. Sunshine that provides energy for plant growth is part of the input. Rainfall that drains into a river and then flows toward the sea is part of the output. A bighorn sheep that leaves the desert and climbs into the forested hills is also part of the output.

Every ecosystem is home to a variety of living things. Each of them has its own role in how the ecosystem functions. This role is called its niche. For example, the desert cottontail is a primary consumer that eats cacti, grasses, and mesquite trees. It serves as food for many predators, including foxes and hawks.

A VARIETY OF INSECTS, SUCH AS THE MORMON CRICKET (ANABRUS SIMPLEX), LIVE IN THE SONORAN DESERT.

Each species has its favored habitat, the kind of place where members of that species can survive and reproduce. The habitat of the desert cottontail is the arid desert lands and short-grass prairies of western North America, from Mexico northward into Montana.

The most important thing about looking at an ecosystem is seeing how everything that happens affects the system as a whole. In a healthy ecosystem, recycling keeps materials available for the next round of production. The input of energy and materials must be sufficient to fuel production.

Different species of plants and animals live in different deserts. The unique elements present in the southwestern United States combine and interact to form the Sonoran Desert ecosystem, a beautiful and productive part of our planet.

THE DESERT COTTONTAIL (SYLVILAGUS AUDUBONII) IS WELL ADAPTED
TO LIVE IN MANY DIFFERENT ARID ENVIRONMENTS.

NORTH AMERICAN DESERTS

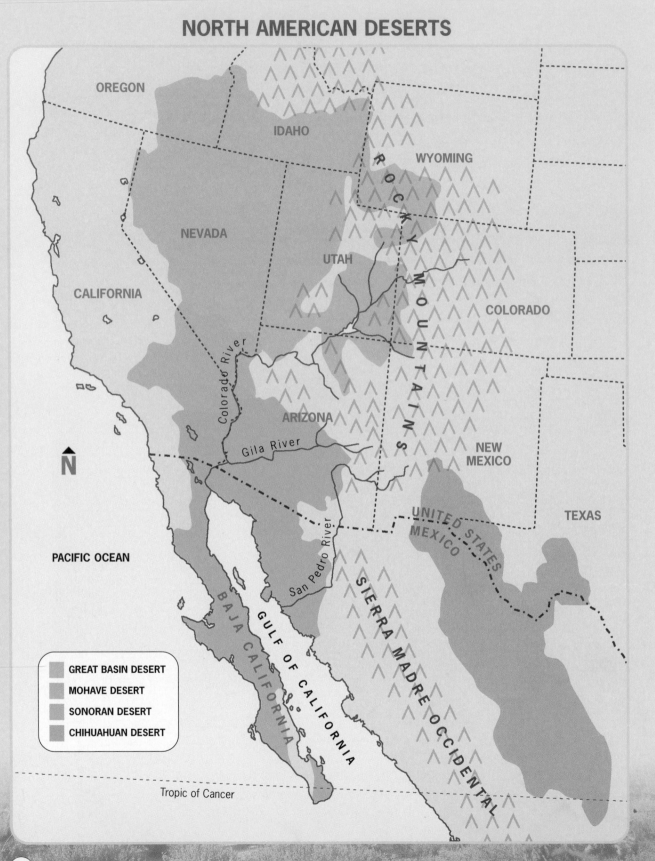

Legend:
- GREAT BASIN DESERT
- MOHAVE DESERT
- SONORAN DESERT
- CHIHUAHUAN DESERT

OREGON

IDAHO

WYOMING

NEVADA

UTAH

CALIFORNIA

COLORADO

ROCKY MOUNTAINS

Colorado River

Gila River

ARIZONA

NEW MEXICO

San Pedro River

TEXAS

UNITED STATES

MEXICO

N

PACIFIC OCEAN

BAJA CALIFORNIA

GULF OF CALIFORNIA

SIERRA MADRE OCCIDENTAL

Tropic of Cancer

CHAPTER 1
THE LIVELIEST DESERT

Does the word *desert* conjure up bare sand dunes burning in the hot sun, with maybe a cactus here and there? Some deserts may be rather bare sand dunes, but not the Sonoran Desert of the American Southwest. The Sonoran Desert is teeming with life—thousands of kinds of plants and hundreds of kinds of animals live there.

So what is a desert? A desert is often defined as a place that receives less than 10 inches (25 centimeters) of rain a year. This definition, however, doesn't really work. For example, the North Slope of Alaska gets less than 10 inches of rain in an average year, but it is covered by tundra, not desert. Part of southern Arizona receives about 12 inches (30 centimeters) of rain a year, but it is a classic desert.

More important than the amount of rainfall is the aridity, or dryness. Aridity is a measure of how fast water evaporates in a particular area. Southern Arizona is so hot and dry that as much as 100 inches (250 centimeters) of rain would evaporate in a year if the place got that much. So the rain that does fall evaporates very quickly, making the area a hot, dry, desert environment.

THE SONORAN DESERT IS HOME TO A GREAT VARIETY OF PLANTS.

Deserts are found all over the world where the sun's rays are strong and the air is dry. The largest desert on Earth is the Sahara Desert in Africa. Other major deserts include the Arabian Desert on the Arabian Peninsula, the Gobi Desert in Asia, the Australian Desert in Australia, and the Patagonian Desert in South America.

NORTH AMERICAN DESERTS

It may seem that deserts are places where few living things can survive, but the Sonoran Desert of the American Southwest is home to a great variety of life. This fascinating ecosystem covers about 100,000 square miles (260,000 square kilometers). It takes up the southwestern third of Arizona and a bit of southeastern California, and it extends southward into Baja California and the district of Sonora in Mexico.

North America has three other major deserts. The Chihuahuan Desert occupies north-central Mexico and extends partway into New Mexico and Texas. The Mojave Desert lies just north of the Sonoran Desert and occupies lowlands in California, Nevada, and a bit of Arizona. The Great Basin Desert is much bigger than the other three. It takes up most of Nevada and Utah as well as southeastern Oregon, southern Idaho, and parts of Wyoming, Colorado, New Mexico, and Arizona.

Not all deserts are hot year-round. Parts of the Great Basin Desert can get very cold in winter, with temperatures below freezing for weeks on end. Most precipitation in the Great Basin Desert comes in the form of winter snow. This is the sagebrush desert, home of plants and animals that can take the cold as well as the heat. The Mojave Desert can also get cold in the winter, with freezes being common. But since it is farther south and therefore warmer, its precipitation comes as cold winter rain. The Chihuahuan Desert extends the farthest south. But because it is relatively high above sea level and cold air from the north can come to it, winter there can also bring freezing temperatures. Since the Chihuahuan Desert is in the path of summer storms, it gets its rain in the summer.

THE SONORAN DESERT

Of all the American deserts, only the Sonoran has mild winters. Frost is rare, which allows for a greater variety of plant life. Many Sonoran plants are related to tropical plant species. The Sonoran Desert is easy to recognize because it is home to very tall cacti, including the giant saguaro. Many trees belonging to the legume, or bean, family also live there. Most are small shrubs, but some, such as velvet mesquite, grow to 40 feet (12 meters) in height. Many legume trees grow only in the Sonoran Desert.

The saguaro cactus and the legume trees can survive in the Sonoran Desert because of its special rain pattern. In the winter, storms come in from the North Pacific Ocean, bringing gentle rains.

THE SONORAN DESERT IS EASY TO RECOGNIZE BECAUSE IT IS HOME TO VERY TALL CACTI, INCLUDING THE GIANT SAGUARO.

Summertime means violent thunderstorms, accompanied by heavy monsoon rains. With rain likely during two seasons, Sonoran plants don't need to survive many, many months without moisture. The two periods of rainfall combined with the mild winters provide an environment that is home to many more species of plants and animals than live in other deserts.

The amount of rainfall through the year, however, varies a great deal in different parts of the Sonoran Desert. Southern Arizona usually gets more than 10 inches (25 centimeters) a year. Farther west, the Sonoran Desert gets only about 3 inches (8 centimeters).

The Sonoran Desert is far from flat. Its elevation ranges from sea level to more than 4,000 feet (over 1,000 meters) above sea level.

Forested mountains run through it, nourished by clouds that release rain when they encounter the mountains. Rocky canyons carry water from the mountains down to the desert. The canyons open up into temporary waterways called arroyos. The arroyos lead to shallower waterways. These temporary waterways of the plain, which are dry more often than the arroyos, are called washes. When rainfall is abundant, water carries rocks and gravel through the arroyos and washes and deposits them on the bare desert floor. These areas of deposited material are called alluvial fans. Over time, the sides of the alluvial fans have merged to create an area of uplands that are called bajadas. Below the bajadas lie the level desert plains. Sometimes it's hard to see the border between the two, but the soil of the bajadas is coarser than that of the plains, where the sand dunes lie. Because they receive more water than the plains, the bajadas show a greater variety of life. Cacti thrive there, as do bushy shrubs and small trees. In the springtime, vast stretches of the bajadas may be covered by brightly blooming wildflowers.

ARROYOS CARRY PRECIOUS WATER DOWN FROM THE MOUNTAINS. THEY SPREAD OUT INTO ALLUVIAL FANS AS THE SLOPE BECOMES LESS STEEP.

All these variations in elevation, rainfall, soil type, and temperature mean that the Sonoran Desert offers a great variety of different ecological niches for living things. No two living things occupy exactly the same ecological niche. Two related birds, such as the ash-throated flycatcher and the brown-crested flycatcher, may live in the same area. Both flycatchers live in the Sonoran Desert and look very similar. Both feed mainly on insects. The ash-throated flycatcher, however, prefers to live along the edge of the woodlands, where it sits on dead branches of trees, then picks insects off of nearby leaves. It nests in cavities in the trees. The brown-crested flycatcher builds its nest in holes made by woodpeckers, in saguaro cacti if possible. It will pick flying insects from the air as well as from leaves. Both species also eat lizards and cactus fruit, but the ash-throated flycatcher includes spiders and berries in its diet.

SONORAN PLANTS

Almost all ecosystems on the earth are fueled by energy from the sun, and plants are the organisms with the equipment to capture that energy. Plants are green when they are growing because of a complicated chemical called chlorophyll in the plants' cells. Chlorophyll soaks up the sun's energy. The plant cells then convert the sun's energy into chemical energy through a set of chemical reactions called photosynthesis. First, the energy is trapped in special energy-rich molecules. Then that energy is used to combine water and carbon dioxide to make molecules of sugar. The chemical energy in the sugars is the energy source

BROWN-CRESTED FLYCATCHER
(MYIARCHUS TYRANNULUS)

for all the plant's activities. The energy can be stored for later use as sugars or as other carbohydrates, such as starch. Or the energy can be burned to fuel growth.

Photosynthesis does more than capture sunlight into a form that can be used by living things. Oxygen is also released during photosynthesis. Most animals need oxygen to fuel their own energy-producing chemical reactions. Some bacteria and a few other life-forms can live without oxygen and have ways of obtaining energy other than through photosynthesis. But without this amazing process, there would be little life on the earth beyond microscopic, single-celled organisms.

CONSERVING WATER

The Sonoran Desert provides plants with plenty of bright sunlight for photosynthesis. These plants don't need to have lots of big leaves to capture enough of the sun's energy. Instead they need ways to protect themselves from too much heat. The vast majority of desert plants have very small leaves or no leaves

at all. And those with leaves drop them when water is scarce.

In some parts of the Sonoran Desert, air temperatures can reach 120 degrees Fahrenheit (49 degrees Celsius). The surface of the ground can be 180 degrees Fahrenheit (82 degrees Celsius) or even more. The heat, combined with the dryness of the air, sucks moisture from both the ground and from the plants themselves.

Some desert plants, such as mesquite trees, deal with scarce rainfall by putting down deep roots that tap into water far below the surface. Others, such as cacti, have dense mats of shallow roots that soak up rain as soon as it falls, before it penetrates deeply into the ground. Many desert plants have nine times as much root material underground as they have stems and leaves above the ground.

To help control the loss of water, cacti have given up completely on leaves, while desert shrubs and bushes have small leaves or almost no leaves at all. Some, such as the ocotillo, have long stems and small leaves. During dry spells, the leaves drop off, and the sturdy stems of some of the leaves form spines. New leaves can sprout from the base of each spine. Within three days of a summer rain, the ocotillo can produce full-grown leaves to take advantage of the brief period of moisture. Other desert shrubs, such as the paloverde, also drop their small leaves during the dry season, but they grow them back only in the cool springtime. Silvery leaves that reflect away some of the strong sunlight and furry leaves that protect against the intense sun are also common on desert plants.

Two related kinds of plants that live on the higher parts of the Sonoran Desert use a completely different tactic for conserving water. These are the agaves and the yuccas. Their stems are so short that the thick, tough leaves form a tight cluster. Agaves and yuccas both bloom by sending up a spectacular tall flowering stalk from the center of the plant. Agave flowers attract all sorts of pollinators, including moths, hummingbirds, and bats. Pollinators carry pollen from the male parts of one flower to the female parts of another. In the flower, the male cell nuclei from the pollen unite

(ABOVE) **AGAVE (AGAVE)**

(LEFT) **OCOTILLO (FOUQUIERIA SPLENDENS)**

with female egg cells. This marks the beginning of the seeds that will become the next generation. Each kind of yucca, however, has its own special species of moth that pollinates only that species of yucca.

DESERT WILDFLOWERS

Water brings life to the Sonoran Desert in a more spectacular way than just about anywhere else. Perennial plants—plants that live for a number of years—need adaptations such as small leaves, thick waxy leaves called cuticles, or deep roots to be able to survive in very hot, dry conditions. Annual desert wildflowers—plants that live less than one year—use a sit-and-wait strategy. Their seeds lie in the soil, sometimes for years, until heavy rains fall. The seeds then germinate, or begin to grow, and quickly produce leaves and flowers while there is still moisture in the soil. At such times, the Sonoran Desert shows breathtaking beauty, with giant clumps of purple, white, and orange blossoms stretching in all directions.

Most annual desert wildflowers bloom in March or April. A soaking rain of 1 inch (3 centimeters) or so during the cool autumn will cause many of their seeds to germinate. Others remain in the soil, insurance in case not enough rain falls in winter and spring to allow the seedlings to survive.

Each seedling produces a small, inconspicuous cluster of leaves that hugs the ground. Then it grows slowly through

THE HEDGEHOG CACTI (ECHINOCEREUS) LIVING IN THE SONORAN DESERT ARE USUALLY NO MORE THAN 1 FOOT (0.3 METER) TALL.

the winter. When the warmth of spring arrives, the plants rush to form flowers. If there has been only modest rainfall, each plant remains small, producing just one flower. But when rain has been abundant, each plant soaks up the sunshine and the water and grows into a healthy, bushy plant with many flowers.

Sometimes a single species dominates. In 1998, desert sunflowers produced a brilliant yellow blanket over an area 40 miles (60 kilometers) long and 10 miles (20 kilometers) wide in southeastern California. It had been twenty years since the last such display.

Elsewhere in the Sonoran Desert, a variety of different species grow near one another. Yellow, orange, pink, purple, blue, and white blooms form colorful tapestries that blanket the desert for a few short weeks.

How can so many wildflower species share what looks like just one kind of habitat? It turns out that a landscape that looks uniform can actually contain a variety of niches. Along a desert wash, for example, fine silt that was carried and deposited by rainwater can lie right next to more gravelly volcanic cinder. When the grand display of flowers blooms, a band of one kind of flower that grows well in silt will bloom right next to a band of a flower that grows well in gravel, with no mingling of the two. For example, the white-blossomed dune evening primrose roots in loose sand, while the rich blue desert bell prefers gravelly soil.

The mix of wildflower species also varies from year to year, as each has its own germination requirements. Desert wildflower seeds contain chemicals that

WHEN ENOUGH RAIN HAS FALLEN, BEAUTIFUL WILDFLOWERS CARPET THE GROUND AROUND DESERT CACTI AND SHRUBS.

keep them from germinating until a particular combination of temperature and moisture occurs. The conditions one year will favor germination and growth of one mix of flowers, while in another year the conditions will cause a different combination to prevail.

While late winter and early spring offer the most spectacular displays of wildflowers, the summer rains bring on another season of bloom. Those species that blossom in the summer, such as summer poppies and morning glories, are a different collection than the spring bloomers, such as Mexican gold poppies and Coulter's lupine.

SONORAN ANIMALS

All sorts of animals live in the Sonoran Desert, from spiders and insects to snakes and lizards, birds and mammals, and even frogs and toads. Each species has developed a variety of ways to conserve water and avoid too much heat.

Animals have an easier time of it than plants do in the desert, since they can move from place to place. Many desert animals spend the daytime in underground burrows, under rocks, or in cavities in the stems of saguaros. When the temperature cools in late afternoon, they come out to feed.

Many desert animals are omnivores. That means that they will eat both plants and animals, making them both primary and secondary consumers. Omnivores are able to take advantage of whatever food sources come along. After a rain, when plants put forth leaves and flowers, omnivores eat them. But when plant food is scarce, they can search out animals for food instead.

A great variety of insects and other invertebrates live in the Sonoran Desert. Ants make underground nests that stay cool. Beetles can find protection among the tangled twigs of desert bushes. Bees, flies, butterflies, and beetles help pollinate desert flowers. Spiders, including tarantulas, hunt for prey, as do scorpions and predatory beetles.

The Sonoran Desert is home to a variety of snakes and lizards. Unlike birds and mammals, reptiles don't have a constant body temperature. When it is cold, their bodies must be warmed by the sun so they can be active. A desert is the perfect home for an animal that depends on the warmth of its surroundings for survival.

Reptiles are adapted to desert life in a number of ways. Since they don't expend energy to keep their body temperature constant, they need a lot less food than do mammals and birds. A snake, tortoise, or lizard can spend long periods of time hidden away in a burrow. As they rest, their bodies use up little energy. Most desert reptiles come out at night, when the harsh sun has set and the sand and rocks are warm, not blazing hot.

Some lizards can store water in their bodies. Gila monsters, chuckwallas, and some geckos have fat tails that can hold water. The tough scales that cover reptiles' skin and the thick shell of the desert tortoise also help reduce water loss.

Most amphibians, such as frogs and toads, are animals that need plenty of moisture, but several species of amphibians live in the Sonoran Desert.

DESERT ANIMALS, SUCH AS THE DESERT TARANTULA *(APHONOPELMA CHALCODES)* (LEFT) AND THE GILA MONSTER *(HELODERMA SUSPECTUM)* (RIGHT), HAVE SPECIAL WAYS OF ADAPTING TO HEAT AND DRYNESS.

They are active, however, only when there has just been a heavy rain. Most desert amphibians spend most of their lives buried in the ground, waiting for the rains.

PLANT DEFENSES

Food is scarce for the primary consumers of the desert, and most desert plants have ways to protect themselves from being eaten. Spines and thorns are especially common defenses. Some cacti have so many spines that the stems themselves are barely visible. Many desert shrubs have spines or thorns, too. The catclaw is a shrub that gets its name from its abundant sharp, hooked spines.

Desert palms such as the California fan palm grow at oases, places in the desert with water springs. Their leaf stalks have rows of tiny pointed spikes to deter browsers. Tough stems and leaves are another deterrent to being eaten.

Distasteful or poisonous chemicals are another common defense of desert plants. The creosote bush, also called greasewood because of the oily shine on its leaves, is the most common shrub growing in the desert Southwest. After rain, the creosote bush produces a pungent scent. The chemicals in its leaves keep just about every desert mammal except the jackrabbit from eating it.

CHAPTER 2

CACTI AS TREES

Many modest-sized cacti live in the Sonoran Desert, but tall cacti are its trademark. The organ-pipe cactus and the senita can grow to be more than 10 feet (3 meters) tall, the size of small trees. In southern parts of the Sonoran Desert, the cardón grows taller than 60 feet (20 meters) in some places. The giant saguaro, the signature plant of the Sonoran Desert in Arizona, often tops 40 feet (12 meters).

While the saguaro has one main stem that gets quite tall before branching, the organ-pipe, senita, and cardón cacti branch low down. The organ-pipe cactus actually has a group of stems that grow directly from ground level. Only a few of the stems develop branches. The senita looks similar to the organ-pipe cactus, but its stems branch low to the ground. The cardón looks similar to a saguaro but has an

(ABOVE) **SAGUARO CACTI (*CARNEGIEA GIGANTEUS*)**

(LEFT) **ORGAN-PIPE CACTUS (*STENOCEREUS THURBERI*)**

abundance of low branches. It is also called the elephant cactus because of its massive size.

THE GIANT SAGUARO

The saguaro is the most abundant and ecologically important cactus of the Sonoran Desert. Saguaros are the tallest cacti in the United States and are found only in the Sonoran Desert. One giant measured 78 feet (25 meters) tall. Saguaros are most abundant in the uplands of Arizona, but they are found all the way from sea level up to about 4,000 feet (over 1,000 meters) in elevation.

The saguaro is tall enough and its stems and arms are thick enough that it takes on the same ecological role as trees do in a forest. The saguaro provides nesting and perching sites for birds. The pollen and nectar from the saguaro's blossoms feed insects, bats, and birds, and its juicy fruits are sought by a great variety of animals including foxes, squirrels, and ants.

A saguaro starts out as a tiny black seed. When a bird eats saguaro fruit, the seeds are not digested. They come out when the bird defecates. Most birds defecate while they are perched in a tree or bush, so the seed lands where there is vital shade to protect a tiny cactus plant from the fierce, drying heat of the sun. A plant that protects a young saguaro is called a nurse plant.

The vast majority of baby saguaros do not survive for long. They are eaten by rabbits, mice, birds, or other animals, or

MANY BIRDS, SUCH AS THE ASH-THROATED FLYCATCHER (*MYIARCHUS CINERASCENS*) NEST IN SAGUAROS IN THE SONORAN DESERT INSTEAD OF IN TREES.

they die from the heat or cold. Almost all of the few that survive lie in the protection of nurse plants, where they are sheltered from the weather and are hard for primary consumers to find. Paloverde trees, which can be 20 to 40 feet (6 to 12 meters) tall, are among the most common nurse plants for saguaros in the Sonoran Desert. Paloverdes are members of the legume family, like most Sonoran Desert bushes and trees. Most other desert plants also depend on nurse plants to protect them during their early years. Only a few, such as the creosote bush and bursage, can become established in exposed places without the protection of a nurse plant.

Conditions in most years are too harsh for the little saguaros. Only once every few decades do a significant number of saguaros survive. The desert landscape has a group of saguaros at about 6 feet (2 meters) tall, another group a few feet taller, and others a few feet taller yet. There are very few plants at heights between the groups. When the surviving plants were seedlings, there were a few years of summers that were wetter than normal and winters that were milder. Saguaros that began their lives under those conditions were much more likely to survive. Since saguaros grow very slowly, these cacti will grow above the height of their nurse plants when they are about fifty years old. By then, their rate of growth will be faster than it was when they were younger. The bigger the plant, the easier it is for it to survive the difficult conditions of desert life.

CONDITIONS IN MOST YEARS ARE TOO HARSH FOR THE LITTLE SAGUAROS. ONLY ONCE EVERY FEW DECADES DO A SIGNIFICANT NUMBER OF SAGUAROS SURVIVE.

PRIMARY PRODUCER/KEYSTONE SPECIES:
IRONWOOD *(Olneya tesota)*

Next to cacti, trees and bushes belonging to the legume family are the most ecologically important plants in the Sonoran desert. Desert ironwood is considered a keystone species for the Sonoran desert. A keystone species is one that influences the lives of many other inhabitants of the ecosystem in important ways. Ironwood is important to more than five hundred species of Sonoran desert organisms that live in its shade, nest in its branches, or feed on its rather soft-shelled seeds.

Ironwood usually keeps its leaves year-round, so it provides consistent shade and cover for plants and animals that live around its base. At up to 35 feet (11 meters) in height, ironwood is often the tallest tree around, providing roosting sites for desert birds. As they eat, the birds drop seeds and fruit from their perches, thus helping feed ground dwellers below. When the seeds fall in the shade of the ironwood tree, they are more likely to germinate than they would out on the hot, dry sand. Seedlings that sprout in an ironwood's shade are protected from primary consumers by the tree's thorny, dense branches. Ironwood serves as a nurse plant for at least 165 other species of plants.

Cacti especially benefit from the nurse plant role of the ironwood. Frost can kill tender young cactus plants, but the temperature beneath an ironwood can be about 7 degrees Fahrenheit (4 degrees Celsius) warmer than the surrounding desert. That can be enough to keep young cacti from freezing. The ironwood's shade also protects the young cacti from too much hot, burning sunlight.

A saguaro begins to grow arms when it is fifty to one hundred years old. Cacti that get more moisture seem to be more likely to grow plenty of arms. A rare saguaro has as many as fifty arms, but some never grow any arms at all. The arms all grow upward, just like the stem. Frost, however, can damage an arm and make it droop. As the plant recovers from the damage, the tip of the arm grows upward again.

Saguaros bloom for the first time when they are about 8 feet (over 2 meters) tall. In wetter parts of the desert, a saguaro begins to bloom when it is about forty years old. Those in drier areas don't flower until they are seventy or seventy-five years old.

Saguaros bloom from late April to June, after being nourished by the winter rains. Their white flowers, each of which is about 3 inches (8 centimeters) in diameter, grow in clusters on the tips of the stems and arms. They open a few hours after sunset, when the air has cooled. By the next afternoon, the flowers that opened during the night are wilting in the heat and have finished blooming.

Many animals visit the saguaro flowers, which smell like overripe melons. Bats visit them during the night, while bees and birds, such as white-winged doves, come by day. These animals feed on the pollen and nectar. When they move on to another flower, they transfer the pollen to that flower, pollinating it.

SAGUARO (CARNEGIEA GIGANTEUS) FLOWERS DON'T ALL OPEN AT THE SAME TIME.

PRIMARY PRODUCERS: CACTI

Cacti are the plants most associated in people's minds with the desert. Cacti are relatives of the rose family that evolved in the Americas. They have adapted to scarce water and aridity in several ways. For one thing, they have given up on leaves. Instead, the chlorophyll in their stems and arms does the work of making food.

In general, cacti are rounded in shape. A round shape has the least surface area for the plant's volume, which helps minimize water loss from the surfaces of the plant. Some cacti, such as prickly pear (Opuntia) species, are flattened, but their pads are still quite thick.

The saguaro and some other cacti have pleated stems and arms, which allow the plant to swell with water when moisture is available and shrink in size as they use the water. The shallow roots of most cacti soak up water rapidly after a rain. It takes only a few hours for them to grow tiny root branches that increase the surface area for gathering moisture. When the ground dries up, these little root branches disappear.

A thick, waxy layer called a cuticle covers the surface of the cactus plant. The cuticle helps prevent water loss. It is often thicker on the sunny side of the plant. Plants have tiny pores in their surface called stomata. The stomata let gases in and out of the plant. Water also can pass out through the stomata. Most plants open their stomata during the day, when they take in carbon dioxide. But cacti close theirs during the hot daytime when they could lose too much water. Instead, they open their stomata at night.

Cacti have spines instead of leaves. The spines serve several functions. They help shade the cactus from the sun's rays. They cut down air currents close to the stem, thereby reducing water loss. Spines can also soak up water when it rains. Finally, the spines protect the plant from animals that might eat it.

Cactus spines grow from special spots called areoles. No other plants have them. The roots, branches, flowers, and fruit also grow from the areoles. Areoles are found on the sides of prickly pear pads and on the ridges of the pleats of cacti such as the saguaro.

About three hundred species of cacti live in the Sonoran Desert. One group of cacti that is especially prevalent in the Sonoran desert is the opuntas. Opuntas include the prickly pears and the chollas. These cacti differ from others in a number of ways. Instead of having a main stem that continues to grow throughout the plant's life, opunta stems consist of a chain of jointed segments. They also have clusters of special tiny bristles called glochids that easily detach from the plant. The glochids are so small they look like bunches of fuzzy fur, but they are actually miniature, nasty spines that easily pierce the skin.

Prickly pears are easy to recognize, with their chains of flat pads instead of rounded stems. Prickly pears serve as food for many desert animals, including javelinas and pack rats. Pack rats often build their nests at the base of prickly pears.

The teddy bear cholla (*Opuntia bigelovii*) and jumping cholla (*Opuntia fulgida*) are both common in parts of the Sonoran Desert. Despite its name, the teddy bear cholla comes with a nasty surprise. It has especially dense spines ready and waiting for a passing animal just to touch them. The barbs grab onto the unfortunate creature, and a joint of stem comes with them. By the time the animal manages to dislodge the cactus, it is some distance from the parent plant. The joint lands on the ground and grows roots to become a new cactus plant. The jumping cholla possesses fewer spines but has the same habit. Both of these cacti can form large, dense forests made up of genetically identical clones that have grown from these dislodged joints.

PRICKLY PEAR CACTI (*OPUNTIA*), WITH THEIR FLAT PADS, ARE TYPICAL DESERT PLANTS.

The pollinated flowers mature into bright red fruit in June and early July. Each fruit contains as many as two thousand seeds. Saguaro fruit is very juicy. It ripens during the hottest, driest time of year, so it provides a vital source of water as well as food for desert animals. Many kinds of birds, mammals, and insects depend on saguaro fruit to get them through this difficult time of year.

SURVIVING IN THE HOT, DRY DESERT

A plant that can live for more than 150 years in the harsh desert must have special ways of coping with the environment. Although a young saguaro is very sensitive to both heat and cold because of its small size, it becomes more and more able to tolerate climate extremes as it grows. The larger a plant is, the less surface area it has relative to its volume. This means that the bigger the saguaro is, the easier it is for it to retain water and the harder it is for frost to penetrate the surface of the plant.

When a saguaro gets really big, however, the upper stems become thinner, making old saguaros susceptible to freezing.

The stem and arms of the saguaro have pleats that allow the cactus to swell with water when moisture is available and shrink in size as it uses up the water. Clusters of hard spines, up to 2 inches (5 centimeters) in length, line the ridges of the pleats for the lowest 8 feet (2 meters) of the stem. The rest of the cactus has more flexible bristles higher up. The spines help protect the plant from being eaten. They also provide some shade from the hot sun. The lower trunk of an old saguaro eventually loses its spines but develops a tough, corklike bark instead.

A waxy, protective cuticle coats the saguaro's stem and arms. Under the cuticle are the cells that contain chlorophyll and undergo photosynthesis. Most of the inside of the plant consists of tissue for storing water. After a good rainstorm, more than 90 percent of a saguaro's volume is taken up by stored water. A good-sized saguaro can gain

1 ton (about 1 metric ton) by soaking up the water from a rainstorm. Inside the stem and arms, a special jellylike material holds the water.

Many desert plants grow a deep taproot to bring up water, but not the saguaro. Its taproot doesn't grow much deeper than 2 feet (60 centimeters). Its other roots grow only in the top 3 inches (8 centimeters) of the ground and extend outward about as far as the plant is tall. So a 40-foot-tall (12-meter-tall) saguaro would have roots that extend about 40 feet in each direction, making a circle 80 feet (25 meters) in diameter. The roots wrap themselves around underground rocks, anchoring the plant firmly in the ground.

Water passes quickly through the sandy or rocky soil of the desert, so after a rainfall, the saguaro's roots collect the water at once. Special tiny root hairs grow quickly in response to moisture. They help soak up as much as 200 gallons (nearly 800 liters) of water from a single storm. That's enough water to support the plant for an entire year.

As a saguaro grows, it causes trouble for its nurse plant. Its roots are so good at soaking up moisture that little water remains for the nurse plant that protected the saguaro and allowed it to grow. The saguaro usually outlives the nurse plant.

A HOME FOR MANY

Many consumers of the Sonoran Desert couldn't live there without the saguaro. Gila woodpeckers and gilded flickers (another type of woodpecker) make their homes in the stems and arms of the saguaro. They use their strong beaks to peck out nest cavities. The saguaro responds by making a hard coating over the wall of the cavity. The temperature in the cavities is much lower than out in the hot sunlight, making them good places to raise young.

Woodpeckers make new nest cavities each year, leaving the old ones. Other birds use the old cavities for their homes. Some of these species, such as the purple martin, screech owl, western kingbird, and American kestrel, are also found in other

ecosystems. Others, such as the cactus wren and elf owl, live only in the desert.

The arms of the saguaro also provide nesting sites. Red-tailed hawks make their nests where the arms meet the stem. Cactus wrens also build among the arms. Many birds alight on the arms to rest or to perch while watching for prey. Flycatchers dart out from saguaros to catch insects, while red-tailed hawks survey the land below for mice and other rodents.

Insects also rely on the saguaro for homes and food. Bees nest in abandoned woodpecker nests. Tiny beetles burrow into the stems from the woodpecker nest holes. One small beetle depends on saguaro flowers for its entire life cycle.

The adults feed on grains of pollen, then they lay their eggs. When the eggs hatch, the larvae feed on pollen and dying flowers.

After the saguaro dies, however, is when it provides the most abundant feast for insects and other invertebrate animals. The body of the dead giant provides food for many kinds of decomposers, such as fungi, which in turn serve as food for fly larvae and mites. Predatory insects, spiders, and scorpions feed in turn on the cleanup crew. In one small piece of rotting saguaro, about 1 cubic foot (30,000 cubic centimeters) of tissue, 413 beetles, fly larvae, mites, and other invertebrates were found.

CHAPTER 3
ON AND BELOW THE SURFACE

In the heat of a summer's day, not much life is evident in the Sonoran Desert except for the plants. The temperature at ground level can reach 180 degrees Fahrenheit (82 degrees Celsius) or more, so most of the animals rest under rocks or in burrows awaiting sunset or rainfall to get on with life.

ANTS OF THE DESERT

Ants are among the earth's most successful creatures. They have found ways of thriving in every major ecosystem, including the Sonoran Desert. There are more ants there than any other animal.

In most environments, a single female ant starts a new colony, becoming the only queen that produces the eggs. Among desert ants, however, young queens often cooperate in starting a new colony. To survive in the hot, dry desert, it's vital that the ants make an underground home. Several queens working together can get the job done more quickly.

One reason ants do so well in the Sonoran Desert is that they can gather food while it is abundant and store it in their underground nests. The stored food then lasts through dry times.

Harvester ants collect plant seeds from a large variety of plants. Then they store them in special chambers near the surface, where it's dry and the seeds

> THE TEMPERATURE AT GROUND LEVEL CAN REACH 180 DEGREES FAHRENHEIT (82 DEGREES CELSIUS) OR MORE, SO MOST OF THE ANIMALS REST UNDER ROCKS OR IN BURROWS AWAITING SUNSET OR RAINFALL TO GET ON WITH LIFE.

won't sprout. Seeds make a perfect food, for they will keep for years without rotting, and they are very nutritious. Seeds, however, are also very hard. Harvester ant workers have powerful jaws that can crush the seeds. The workers break them apart and feed bits of the most nutritious parts of the seeds to the colony's larvae. A colony of harvester ants can survive on stored seeds through years of drought.

Harvester ants live in huge colonies. Tens of thousands of workers live in large nests that extend more than 1 yard (1 meter) below the surface. The worker ants go out early in the morning, before daylight, in search of food. When the temperature heats up, they stay in the nest. In the afternoon, after it has begun to cool off, out they go again to resume the search. They look far and wide, with as many as 17,000 workers from one colony stretching out in a column that reaches 45 yards (41 meters) from the entrances to the nest.

Honeypot ants also store the food they gather, but in an entirely different way from that of harvester ants. Two favorite food sources for honeypot ants are flower nectar and a liquid called honeydew. Honeydew is made by insects that suck on plant juices, such as aphids and scale insects. The sugary juice that these insects don't need is excreted at the rear of their bodies. Honeypot ants collect this juice for food. Both flower nectar and honeydew, however, are available for only part of the year.

Honeypot ants have an amazing way of solving their food storage problem. When some of the largest worker ants have just molted into the adult form and their bodies are still soft, they are recruited for a special job—they become living food-storage jars. Other workers give the food they collect to these special workers, called repletes. The food remains stored in the repletes' abdomens until needed by the colony. The repletes hang from the ceiling of the nest chamber and become so swollen with sugary liquid that they are the size of peas. Some repletes are used to store water instead of nutrients. The repletes can live this way for years.

DECOMPOSER: PALOVERDE ROOT BORER
(Derobrachus geminatus)

A vital step in nature's recycling system is the breakdown of plant and animal tissue into simple chemicals that can then be reused by other plants and animals. Fungi, bacteria, and insects do most of this decomposition.

The paloverde root borer is an impressive beetle that can be more than 3 inches (8 centimeters) long. The female beetle lays her eggs on the shallow roots of paloverde bushes and other trees. When the eggs hatch, tiny grublike larvae crawl out. Right away, the larvae eat their own egg shells.

By doing so, they ingest a host of bacteria and other microorganisms that help them digest wood. The larvae burrow into the roots and eat their way through them. The microorganisms living in their guts digest the tough cellulose in the roots, turning it into chemicals the larvae's bodies can use. As the larvae grow, they shed

their protective outer skin several times, eventually reaching 5 inches (13 centimeters) in length. Then they shed their skin for the last time and become pupae. Fully formed adult beetles grow inside the pupae and then break their way out.

Many insects, including other beetles and termites, as well as cattle, deer, goats, and many other plant-eating mammals, also harbor microorganisms in their digestive systems. These microorganisms help them digest cellulose and thereby contribute to natural recycling.

Honeypot ant colonies are large. One colony was found to contain a single queen and about 15,000 worker ants, including 1,500 repletes, in a nest that extended 17 feet (5 meters) into the desert soil.

DESERT SPIDERS AND SCORPIONS

Most familiar spiders spin webs, often beautiful orbs that gather morning dew. In the desert, however, most spiders live in or close to the ground, where they are more protected from desert heat and dryness. They tend to be active at night, when it's cooler. Brown spiders and funnel-web spiders make webs close to the ground for catching prey. Other spiders catch prey in different ways.

Trap-door spiders build silk-lined underground tunnels where insects are likely to pass by. A hinged silken door, camouflaged to look like the desert floor, tops the tunnel. When hunting, the trap-door spider waits just below the door. It can feel the vibrations of a passing insect. When the insect is nearby, the spider throws open the tunnel door, snatches the prey, and retreats into its tunnel to feed.

Tarantulas are the most familiar desert spiders. The desert tarantula lives in the Sonoran Desert. Male desert tarantulas are 2.0 to 2.6 inches (5.0 to 6.6 centimeters) and females are up to 4 inches (10 centimeters) in diameter. Despite their fearsome appearance, the bite of the desert tarantula is usually no worse than a bee sting. These spiders rarely attack animals other than their prey.

Desert tarantulas live in burrows, coming out at night to feed nearby. In winter, the spider plugs the entrance to its burrow and lives off stored fat until the weather warms up.

The scorpion is another venomous desert animal. It has a sharp stinger on the tip of its tail. Scorpions use their stingers on the insects they eat or on predators that attack them. Of the more than thirty kinds of scorpions living in Arizona, only two produce poison that is life threatening to large animals. Scorpions spend the day hidden under rocks or in other protected places, coming out at night to hunt.

DESERT REPTILES

Many kinds of lizards live in the Sonoran Desert. Some, such as the Gila monster, chuckwalla, and desert iguana, also live in other deserts. But others, such as the regal horned lizard and Sonoran fringe-toed lizard, are found only in the Sonoran Desert.

The regal horned lizard, like other horned lizards, has a flattened body and short tail. It has ten horns at the base of its head. This dragonlike creature is about 5 inches (13 centimeters) long and can lighten or darken the color of its gray-and-tan body to match its surroundings. Its favorite food consists of the abundant harvester ants of the Sonoran Desert.

The 5-to-7-inch-long (13-to-18-centimeter-long) fringe-toed lizard has fringelike scales on the back edges of its hind feet that act like snowshoes to keep the lizard from sinking in the sand. It also has special adaptations that allow it to burrow into dunes to avoid predators and heat. It can close off its nose to keep out

SCORPIONS (SCORPIONES), SUCH AS THIS ONE (HADRURUS), ARE FOUND
IN ALL THE DESERTS OF THE UNITED STATES.

the sand. And it has scaly flaps that protect its ears from the sand, as well as overlapping eyelids to protect its eyes.

The chuckwalla is a large lizard, 11 to 18 inches (28 to 46 centimeters) in length, with loose skin around its neck and shoulders. It lives among rocks and large boulders. In the morning it comes out to sun itself. When its body reaches about 100 degrees Fahrenheit (38 degrees Celsius), it heads out to look for fruit, leaves, and flowers to eat. If alarmed, it dashes into a crevice and fills its body with air, wedging itself in safely so it can't be budged.

The Gila monster and the Mexican beaded lizard are the only poisonous lizards in the world. The Mexican beaded lizard lives in parts of Mexico and Guatemala. But the Gila monster prefers to live in gravelly areas of the Sonoran Desert, where it digs its own burrow or lives in a burrow abandoned by another animal. Its skin is covered with patches of black-and-orange, pink, or yellow scales. The scales are small and beadlike.

The Gila monster's chunky body, heavy tail, and short, thick legs help it conserve water by giving it less surface area for the size of its body. This calm, slow-moving animal uses its poison to overpower its prey or any predators foolish enough to tackle it. The poison is produced by glands in the lower jaw, and it flows into a victim's wounds through grooves on the Gila monster's teeth.

A variety of snakes, too, are commonly seen in deserts.

CHUCKWALLAS (SAUROMALUS) LIVE IN BOTH THE SONORAN AND MOJAVE DESERTS.

SECONDARY CONSUMER: SPADEFOOT TOAD
(*Scaphiopus* species)

Amphibians such as frogs and salamanders have thin skins that usually need to be kept moist, so they are not well adapted to life in the desert. Spadefoot toads solve this problem by spending most of their adult lives underground. Their hind feet have special tough projections that allow them to dig as far as 3 feet (1 meter) deep. Once buried, the toads can stay in a state of rest, living mostly on stored fat, for up to nine months.

COUCH'S SPADEFOOT TOAD (*SCAPHIOPUS COUCHI*)

When rains are heavy, the toads come to the surface at twilight and gather at ponds to mate. The males call loudly to attract the females. The females then lay long strings of eggs that the males fertilize. The tadpoles hatch in a matter of hours. It's a race with time for them to feed, grow, and develop into tiny toads before the pond dries up. Most tadpoles feed on algae, but spadefoot tadpoles are predators, feeding on mosquito larvae and on one another. Animal food is much more energy-rich than algae, speeding the tadpoles' growth. Within ten days, the spadefoot tadpoles have become miniature toads. Five or six of them would fit on the surface of a dime.

The little spadefoot toads still have tails when they leave the water. Soon the tails are absorbed into their bodies. The toads grow quickly, nourished by the abundant insect life encouraged by the rains. If all goes well, those that survive heat and predators will be well enough nourished to dig down deep into the ground and remain there until the storms come again.

Many desert snakes, including the longnose snake, the ground snake, and the shovel-nosed snake, have bodies banded with yellow, red, and black. These bright patterns make the snakes obvious, but there's a reason for that. The poisonous Arizona coral snake also has yellow, red, and black bands. By looking like a poisonous snake, these nonpoisonous snakes make predators think twice before trying to attack them.

Several kinds of poisonous rattlesnakes live in the Sonoran Desert. Some kinds, such as the speckled rattlesnake, vary their activity depending on the season. The speckled rattlesnake, which lives in rocky areas, comes out only at night during the summer but is active during the day in the cooler spring and fall. The sidewinder rattlesnake is especially adapted to desert life. It uses sideways coils of its body to travel very quickly across sandy areas.

Some Sonoran Desert snakes spend much of their time underground. The spotted leafnose snake has a triangular patch of scales that curve over the tip of its snout. This patch of scales helps the snake to burrow into the ground.

The desert tortoise is a very important resident of the Sonoran Desert. It can grow to a shell length of 15 inches (38 centimeters) and weigh as much as 15 pounds (7 kilograms). Like many other kinds of tortoises, the desert tortoise may live to be one hundred years old.

The desert tortoise eats a variety of plants, including grasses and wildflowers. It gets most of its water from its food, but

THE FRONT LEGS OF THE DESERT TORTOISE (*XEROBATES AGASSIZI*) ARE FLATTENED INTO POWERFUL DIGGING TOOLS.

it also digs pits in the ground that catch rainfall. The tortoise senses when rain is on the way and waits by one of its pits. When the pit fills with rainwater, the tortoise drinks and drinks. Its bladder can store enough water to last for months.

GROUND-NESTING BIRDS

The vast majority of birds that live in the Sonoran Desert spend most of their time above the ground, in bushes, on cacti, or among the branches of trees that live along waterways. One kind of quail, Gambel's quail, is an exception. It nests on the ground near desert waterways.

Cartoons have made the one common ground-nesting bird in the desert, the roadrunner, famous. The roadrunner is up to 2 feet (60 centimeters) long from the tip of its beak to the end of its tail. It would rather walk or run than fly. It can zoom away at 17 miles (27 kilometers) an hour. This black-and-white member of the cuckoo family is especially well adapted for life in the desert. The roadrunner's kidneys are especially efficient and remove large amounts of water from the urine before it is eliminated. Because of this, the roadrunner can survive with less water than most other birds of the same size.

Roadrunners are secondary consumers that eat insects, scorpions, lizards, rodents, and snakes. Roadrunners are very quick hunters, too. They can even attack and kill rattlesnakes. Using its sharp beak, a roadrunner grabs a snake's tail, then snaps it like a whip, banging the snake's head against the ground until it is dead.

THE ROADRUNNER (GEOCOCCYX CALIFORNIANUS) LIVES AMONG THE BUSHES AND SHRUBS OF THE DESERT.

PRIMARY CONSUMER: KANGAROO RAT *(Dipodomys)*

Kangaroo rats are well suited for life in the hot, dry desert. Instead of scurrying about on all fours, they hop from place to place using their large, strong hind legs. They use their long tails for balance. And their long, hairy toes act like snowshoes, keeping the animals from sinking into sandy ground.

Like most other desert animals, kangaroo rats escape from heat and predators by retreating into burrows. Each kangaroo rat has its own burrow, which is actually a network of underground tunnels with up to eight entrances. Kangaroo rats rest during the day within their dens, in a nest area about 2 feet (0.6 meters) deep. The burrow is significantly cooler than the surface. One scientist found that when the air temperature was 103 degrees Fahrenheit (39 degrees Celsius), it was 92 degrees Fahrenheit (33 degrees Celsius) just inside the entrance to one burrow and only 86 degrees Fahrenheit (30 degrees Celsius) 2 feet (0.6 meters) below the surface.

Kangaroo rats come out to feed at night, when it's easier to avoid predators. Their main food is dry seeds, rather than the juicy cactus pads or fruits sought by so many primary consumers of the desert. Despite their dry diet, these amazing creatures never need to drink water. Their bodies are able to manufacture the water they need from the chemicals in the food they eat. They have other ways of conserving water, too. The kangaroo rat blocks the entrances to its nest during the day, which helps preserve the humidity within the nest. In addition, its kidneys are very efficient, removing as much water as possible from its urine.

SONORAN MAMMALS

Because of its varied terrain that includes moist canyons and relatively cool mountains, the Sonoran Desert region is home to many large mammals that are able to move around easily to find a suitable habitat. Coyotes, bobcats, mountain lions, deer, pronghorn, and many other adaptable mammals found elsewhere also live in the Sonoran Desert. The Sonoran Desert is also home to many mammals that are specialized in different ways for life in a hot, dry land.

Rodents, such as pocket mice and kangaroo mice, are typical desert animals. It's easy for such small creatures to find refuge from the heat in burrows or cracks between rocks. Pocket mice can hibernate for long periods when conditions are difficult. Bailey's pocket mouse, which lives on rocky slopes of the Sonoran Desert, carries seeds back to its burrow in its cheek pouches, then stores them for the winter. This species doesn't hibernate like its cousins do.

One very common, relatively small desert mammal, the desert jackrabbit, doesn't retreat to a burrow, even during the hottest days of summer. The desert jackrabbit is actually not a rabbit at all—it's a hare. Hares differ from rabbits in several ways. While baby rabbits are born hairless and blind, jackrabbits come into the world fully furred and with their eyes open. Another big difference between rabbits and hares is their ears. Rabbits have large ears, but a hare's ears are enormous. These ears act as an air-conditioning system. As blood flows through the blood vessels in the ears, it is cooled and returns to the body at a lower temperature.

A jackrabbit spends the hottest part of the day in a simple depression in the ground called a form. The form lies in the shade of bushes or shrubs. The shade helps keep the desert jackrabbit cool, and the surrounding brush and dry grass help to hide the hare and protect it from drying winds.

CHAPTER 4
ALONG THE WATERWAYS

Water is vital to life. Some animals and plants have adapted to the desert's aridity. Others live in the parts of the desert where water is easier to get.

When rain comes, much of it soaks through the sandy ground and renews the water table. The water table is a hidden layer of water that feeds the deepest plant roots and the desert springs. The rest of the water flows through the arroyos and washes, producing ribbons of habitat with somewhat more water than the surrounding desert. The portion of that water that doesn't soak in ends up in the desert's rivers. There it nourishes a great abundance of life along their banks. Finally, when the rivers flow into the sea, their fertile, muddy deltas provide habitat for a dizzying variety of plants and animals, including many whose lives are bound to the sea.

The monsoon rains of summer and the gentle rains of winter bring water to the entire surface of the desert, supplying this vital fluid to animals and plants across the landscape. But more rain falls in the mountains that punctuate the Sonoran Desert than on the desert floor

WATERWAYS SUCH AS THE SANTA CRUZ RIVER ARE VERY IMPORTANT TO THE DIVERSITY OF LIFE IN THE DESERT.

itself. And gravity leads that water downhill, first through the narrow, steep mountain canyons, then out onto the arroyos of the bajada. As water moves along the arroyos and washes, much of the water soaks down through the porous desert sand and soil, but some eventually reaches the major rivers that flow through the region.

Plants and animals that thrive on the availability of precious water live along the desert waterways. Even when the arroyos look dry, the water content of the ground below the surface can be significantly higher than it is on the rest of the desert. About 5 percent of the surface area of the desert is occupied by arroyos. But because of the availability of water, that 5 percent harbors an especially abundant variety of life, including many plants and animals not found elsewhere.

> **EVEN WHEN THE ARROYOS LOOK DRY, THE WATER CONTENT OF THE GROUND BELOW THE SURFACE CAN BE SIGNIFICANTLY HIGHER THAN IT IS ON THE REST OF THE DESERT.**

Several kinds of large bushes and small trees, including the desert willow, smoke tree, and blue paloverde, are inhabitants of the arroyos. The smoke tree is a ghostly looking bush that grows up to 20 feet (6 meters) tall. It appears to be dead for most of the year. The wispy, finely divided twigs give the tree a smoky look from a distance. The smoke tree grows leaves only for a few weeks when the rains come. But the gray-green bark of the fine twigs contains chlorophyll and carries out most of the plant's photosynthesis. Blooming in May, the smoke tree comes alive with clusters of purple, pealike flowers. Rains carry the seeds down the arroyos. Smoke tree seeds will germinate only after being scratched and roughed up as they tumble downstream.

Mesquite trees also grow along arroyos and washes. They can keep their small leaves during the summer because their roots reach down 80 feet (24 meters) to soak up water. At the hottest time of day, the leaves fold together, which helps keep in moisture. Mesquite produces large pods containing nutritious beans, which are a major source of food for many desert animals. Mesquite drops its leaves during the winter, then grows new leaves when it warms up in the spring.

Much of the desert's animal life is concentrated along its waterways. Rodents such as kangaroo rats, pack rats, and ground squirrels make their nests among the debris that collects under the bushes and trees. Predators such as coyotes and kit foxes hunt the rodents. Javelinas, also called collared peccaries, are piglike animals with hooves. They spend up to half their time near arroyos, rooting around for the pods of mesquite and the seeds of other trees. Up to one quarter of their summer diet is made up of the pods of such legumes.

Ninety percent of Sonoran Desert birds live along the waterways. The

JAVELINAS *(DICOTYLES TAJACU)* AVOID THE DESERT HEAT BY BEING ACTIVE IN
THE EARLY MORNING AND LATE AFTERNOON, WHEN THE TEMPERATURE IS COOLER.
PHAINOPEPLAS *(PHAINOPEPLA NITENS)* ARE OFTEN FOUND IN THE SONORAN DESERT,
BUT THEY ACTUALLY PREFER AREAS WITH SINGLE TALL TREES.

phainopepla is a crested flycatcher that has adapted to life in the desert. Female phainopeplas are gray, and males are a beautiful glossy black. Most flycatchers eat only insects, so they retreat south in winter as more northern populations of insects decline. The phainopepla, however, switches its diet in winter and eats the berries of desert mistletoe to get both water and nourishment. Desert mistletoe is a parasite that steals nourishment from bushes and small trees that live along the washes and arroyos. Desert mistletoe produces dense clumps of tiny leaves within the tree branches. Its abundant red berries serve as food for many creatures besides the phainopepla.

Washes also provide passageways for some tropical species of plants and animals to survive farther north than they otherwise would. The Mexican jumping bean grows along washes that snake from the United States into Mexico, as does the tiger rattlesnake.

DESERT CANYONS

In the mountains, streams and creeks rush between canyon walls. Some creeks run year-round, their flow only petering out once they leave the mountains and enter the bajadas. A different assortment of living things inhabits these canyons, including species that must have abundant water, such as frogs. Visitors from the desert, such as coatis and javelinas, also come to the creeks.

THE PHAINOPEPLA AND OTHER BIRDS
FEED ON THE BERRIES OF DESERT MISTLETOE
(PHORADENDRON CALIFORNICUM).

The canyons vary enormously. To the east are dry hills, which do not produce year-round creeks. The mountains to the north and west of the Sonoran Desert, however, are tall and well forested. They receive enough rain to keep streams flowing. As a canyon climbs between the mountains, the kinds of plants and animals change gradually from those adapted to the hot, dry desert to species similar to ones found farther north. Deciduous trees, with large leaves that turn color and drop in the fall, grow here, just as they do in the Northeast and Midwest.

One common tree of these canyons is the western cottonwood. Cottonwoods consume a tremendous amount of water. They suck it up with their roots and let it out from the stomata, or tiny breathing holes, in their leaves. The result is a significant increase in the humidity and lowering of the temperature of the canyons compared to the hot, dry desert. Where cottonwoods grow, insects abound, and with them their predators, such as

skunks and raccoons. Both of these adaptable animals also feed on other foods. Skunks eat mice and the eggs of birds that nest on the ground, while raccoons catch frogs and fish and savor fruits and berries.

At higher elevations, above the realm of the cottonwoods, the mountain environment changes so much that it is no longer much connected to the desert. Plants that tolerate frost live here, where winter nights can be cold. Trees such as oaks grow here too. Higher up, pinyon pines and other evergreens grow. The plants and animals on the mountains have more in common with those that live farther north than they do with the inhabitants of the nearby desert.

OASES IN THE DESERT

Here and there on the desert are natural springs that form pools of water. Such oases provide vital water for many desert plants and animals and are home to some creatures, such as certain fish, that live nowhere else. Desert pupfish live in oasis pools in the Sonoran Desert. They

also live in the rare desert marshes and lakes. The light tan female desert pupfish are less than 2 inches (5 centimeters) long. Males are almost 3 inches (8 centimeters) in length and change from light tan to a brilliant blue during the mating season in spring and early summer.

Pupfish are very tolerant of changes in temperature and the salinity of the water. They can live in freshwater as well as water saltier than the ocean, and can survive water temperatures above 100 degrees Fahrenheit (38 degrees Celsius) and below 50 degrees Fahrenheit (10 degrees Celsius).

Two major rivers, the Gila and the Colorado, drain the basin of the Sonoran Desert. These rivers are home to many different species of fish. Water-loving trees, such as cottonwoods, crowd their shores. Desert animals such as coyotes and mule deer visit rivers to obtain water, and species not normally found in the desert make their homes along their shores. Rivers also provide corridors for tropical plants and animals, such as the green kingfisher, that need water to live farther north than they otherwise would.

A SONORAN DESERT MARSH

CHAPTER 5
BIODIVERSITY

The Sonoran is the most biologically diverse of all American deserts and probably of all the deserts in the world. Twenty different wildflower species can be found in just 1 square yard (0.8 square meter) of ground. In just 1 acre (0.4 hectare) of a cactus forest in southeastern Arizona, up to one hundred different kinds of plants may live.

A great variety of plants leads to animal diversity, especially of pollinators. Seventeen different species of hummingbirds are attracted to wildflowers that bloom in southern Arizona, more than can be found anywhere else in the United States. More than one thousand species of solitary bees—bees that live alone instead of in colonies, as honeybees do—live in southeastern Arizona. That's one fifth of all known native bee species in North America. And the southern canyons harbor more than one hundred kinds of butterflies and even more species of moths.

REASONS FOR DIVERSITY

The Sonoran Desert is especially diverse partly because of its two periods of rainfall each year but also for other reasons.

COSTA'S HUMMINGBIRD (CALYPTE COSTAE)

Within this desert, the amount of rainfall, the elevation above sea level, the composition of the soil or sand, and other factors differ greatly, providing a great variety of habitats.

Along the border between Mexico and the United States is a large gap between the Rocky Mountains of the United States and the Sierra Madre Occidental, the mountain range that forms the spine of Mexico. Instead of closely connected mountains, this region has more isolated peaks. Each peak is separated from its neighbors by the hot, arid desert below, just as islands in the sea are separated by the ocean's waters. These mountaintops have been dubbed the "sky islands," for they harbor "islands" of plant biodiversity that thrives on the cool, moist mountains. Every 1,000 feet (300 meters) in increased elevation is the ecological equivalent of moving about 300 miles (500 kilometers) farther north.

The Sonoran Desert lies at the base of the mountains. As the elevation increases, the desert gives way to the deciduous forest, where trees lose their leaves in winter. Farther up, the pine-spruce forest replaces the deciduous forest. At the very tops of the highest mountains, no trees can grow. Alpine tundra, similar to the arctic tundra of the far north of Alaska, covers the ground. All these different habitats are home to different life-forms. Where one habitat melts into another, plants and animals from both mingle.

Some plants and animals live in only one well-defined area. These species are said to be "endemic," found nowhere else. Island chains, such as the Galápagos Islands and the Hawaiian

THE SONORAN IS THE MOST BIOLOGICALLY DIVERSE OF ALL AMERICAN DESERTS AND PROBABLY OF ALL THE DESERTS IN THE WORLD.

SKY ISLAND

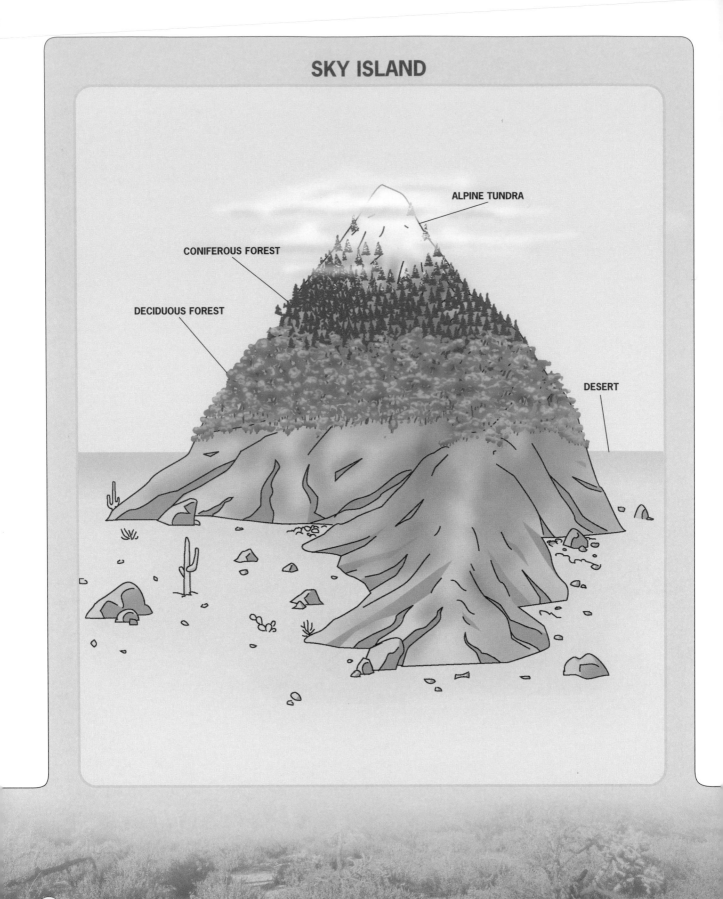

Islands, have many endemic species. A few plants and animals managed to reach the islands by various means. Then they adapted to different conditions on different parts of the islands and evolved into a variety of new species. The Sonoran Desert is home to a number of endemic species, too. In this case, the organisms are so narrowly adapted to life there that they can't survive in other nearby habitats. The section of the Sonoran Desert in Baja California has 552 endemic plant species, species that don't live even in other parts of the Sonoran Desert. There is an especially large number of endemic reptiles—96 species are found only there.

DESERT SUBDIVISIONS

The Sonoran Desert itself can be divided into seven subdivisions, each with its own typical common plant species. Two of these subdivisions of the Sonoran Desert are in the United States—the Lower Colorado River Valley and the Arizona Upland. The other five are limited to Mexico. The plants and animals that live in the subdivisions vary depending on the altitude, slope of the land, and availability of water.

The Lower Colorado River Valley is the driest and hottest of all the subdivisions, as well as being the biggest. So little rain falls here that it is also called the small-leafed desert, since the most common plants are shrubs and bushes with small leaves, which reduce water loss. The two most drought-resistant plants in North America, creosote bush and white bursage, comprise up to 90 percent of the plant life on the valley floor. Various species of chollas are the most common cacti.

CREOSOTE BUSHES *(LARREA TRIDENTATA)* SCENT THE DESERT AIR WITH THEIR SHARP AROMA.

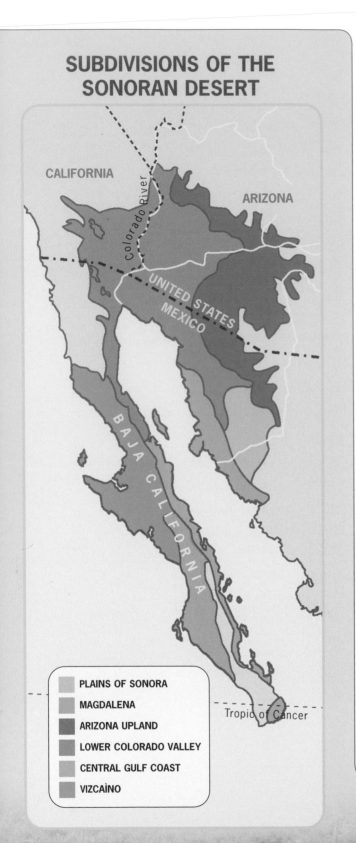

SUBDIVISIONS OF THE SONORAN DESERT

CALIFORNIA

ARIZONA

Colorado River

UNITED STATES
MEXICO

BAJA CALIFORNIA

Tropic of Cancer

- PLAINS OF SONORA
- MAGDALENA
- ARIZONA UPLAND
- LOWER COLORADO VALLEY
- CENTRAL GULF COAST
- VIZCAÍNO

The Arizona Upland subdivision is the coolest part of the Sonoran Desert. It also has the highest mountains, etched by narrow valleys. The Arizona Upland subdivision is also called the paloverde cacti desert. This is the beautiful desert dominated by impressive saguaro cacti. But many other cactus species live here, including chollas, barrel cacti, and prickly pears.

Two kinds of paloverde are common in the Sonoran Desert in the United States. Blue paloverde lives along arroyos and washes over a wide range, while foothill paloverde is common in the Arizona Upland subdivision. Foothill paloverde is a large shrub or small tree that grows to 20 feet (6 meters), while blue paloverde is a tree that can reach 40 feet (12 meters) in height. The name *paloverde* means "green stick." The stems of foothill paloverde are yellowish green, while those of blue paloverde are bluish green. Paloverde is quick to drop its modest leaves when the weather is either too hot and dry or too cool. The green bark carries on photosynthesis, so even when it is leafless, a paloverde bush isn't dormant. During their short period of flowering, paloverdes become covered with yellow blossoms. Twenty different bee species, as well as beetles and flies, may feed at the same time among the blossoms.

TAIL END OF THE TROPICS

The Sonoran is a subtropical desert, with its southernmost portions in Baja California nudging up against the Tropic of Cancer, which is the northern limit of the tropics. This proximity to the tropics is another reason for the great biodiversity of the Sonoran Desert. While tropical plants accustomed to moisture as well as warmth can't survive in the desert, some tropical animals, which can adjust their movements to the ups and downs of climate, are able to live there.

Tropical birds, such as the elegant trogon, visit canyons in southeastern Arizona. Millions of migratory birds headed for the tropics fly along the San Pedro River right by the Sonoran Desert.

Here tropical species, such as the green kingfisher, tropical kingbird, and gray hawk, can be seen. Altogether, more than 380 different species of birds have been identified passing through this area.

Tropical mammals, too, visit the Sonoran Desert. The coati and the javelina are both familiar residents of the tropical rain forests of Central and South America. Both also live successfully along the margins of the Sonoran Desert. They succeed because they are very adaptable, mobile animals that travel to shelter and water to avoid the desert's aridity. They are omnivores that take advantage of whatever food is available. Javelinas eat mostly plants, while coatis eat more animal foods.

Javelinas live in groups of males and females. A group usually consists of five to fifteen animals. Each group has its own home range, with the areas between home ranges being shared with other groups. During the heat of the day, the animals retreat into a shaded, sheltered place. When it is cool, javelinas forage for food, using their snouts and sharp hooves to dig up bulbs and roots as well as insect grubs that

live in the ground. They also munch on juicy cactus fruit and berries and will consume snakes and other small animals.

Coatis tend to stay in the cooler wooded areas along streams. Females and their young live in groups, usually of up to twenty individuals. Adult males tend to live alone. Like so many desert animals, coatis forage for food in the morning and evening. They hunt for food both in trees and on the ground, using their long claws and pointed snouts to uncover insect grubs and other invertebrates that live on or just under the surface of the ground. They also eat mice,

bird and reptile eggs, lizards, dead animals, and berries. Coatis sleep at night, usually in caves or in trees.

VISITORS FROM THE NORTH

Both plants and animals from the cooler north also enrich Sonoran biodiversity. In spring, hundreds of bird species visit the Sonoran Desert on their way north to breed. In the fall, some of them pass through on their way south.

Some birds that breed farther north, however, stop to spend the winter in the desert. The burrowing owl, lark bunting, Brewer's blackbird, and vesper sparrow are examples of birds that spend summers in the north and winters in the region of the Sonoran Desert.

VESPER SPARROW (POOECETES GRAMINEUS)

CHAPTER 6
PEOPLE IN THE SONORAN DESERT

Humans have lived in the Sonoran Desert area for at least twelve thousand years. Since their arrival, they have affected the ecosystem in many ways. Their influence has increased tremendously over time.

NATIVE AMERICANS CHANGE THE DESERT

The Hohokam people settled in Arizona around A.D. 300. They were farmers and hunters. Archeologists have found that the longer the Hohokam lived in a particular area, the fewer large meat animals such as bighorn sheep and pronghorn shared the land with them. As the large animals were hunted out, smaller creatures such as cottontail rabbits and jackrabbits became more numerous.

In order to farm in the desert, the Hohokam had to modify the environment to bring reliable sources of water to their fields. They constructed huge irrigation canals to divert water from rivers and washes to their farms. The Hohokam built the largest irrigation system known to have existed in North America before the arrival of Europeans. Their canals travel up to 315 miles (507 kilometers) from river to farm in the area around present-day Phoenix, Arizona.

The Hohokam and the other Native American groups that followed them grew many different crops. In one area near present-day Tucson, Arizona, the Hohokam grew large numbers of agave plants on rock terraces. The terraces helped to conserve water as well as to protect the young agave plants from mice and other rodents. In the 1100s and 1200s, more than one hundred thousand agave plants may have been grown at one time in this area.

Hohokam culture disappeared abruptly around A.D. 1450. Perhaps the

great floods that occurred in 1353 and the years of drought that followed were to blame for their disappearance. Other peoples followed, especially five major tribes, some of whom survive to this day. The Apache lived in the eastern mountains, while Seri Indians lived along the coast of the Gulf of California. The Pima inhabited the river valleys, and the Yaqui farmed river deltas in the desert. The Papago, who call themselves the Tohono O'odham, took advantage of the different climates found in different areas. They farmed in the valleys in the summer and hunted in the mountains during the winter.

Native farmers brought cultivated plants with them from their original homelands. Cultivation of corn, which originated in Mexico, began at least three thousand years ago in the Sonoran Desert. Indians also grew cotton, squash, various beans, gourds, and other crops.

Native peoples also used desert plants for food, building materials, and medicines. The pads and fruit of the prickly pear were an important food, as were pods from mesquite and other legume family desert plants. Creosote bushes provided medicines to treat many different ailments from cancer to wounds, and from dandruff to postnasal drip. Mesquite, as well as the strong skeletal posts of dead saguaros, provided wood for building.

Desert palms did more than indicate the location of oases and the water they contained. Their buds, flowers, and fruit provided food, and their fronds made good thatching for roofs. Palm fibers were

SEGMENTS OF HOHOKAM CANALS MAY STILL BE SEEN IN PHOENIX. SOME OF THEM STILL CARRY WATER THROUGH THE CITY.

used for making baskets and sandals, and their wood was burned for cooking fires.

EUROPEAN SETTLEMENT

Life changed drastically for native peoples when the Spanish arrived in the early 1600s. First came epidemics of European diseases such as influenza, measles, and smallpox, which killed countless natives. The Spanish also brought many different domesticated animals and new crops such as wheat. Their mules and oxen would help cultivate fields, horses would speed transportation, and cattle, goats, and sheep would provide meat and milk.

The Spanish established missions in the desert to convert the Indians to Christianity. Indians resisted the intrusion of the Spanish until the late 1800s, but eventually the Spanish ruled throughout the Southwest, running thousands of cattle, sheep, horses, and other livestock that overgrazed the delicate desert.

The U.S.-Mexican War of 1846 to 1848 brought over half of Mexico's territory into the United States. Soon other people of European descent joined the Spanish Americans, attracted by the lure of gold and silver. Some Indian tribes continued to fight with the interlopers until the 1880s. The railroad reached Tucson in 1880, ending the Indian era for good. Since then, settlement of the desert has kept increasing. Millions of people now make the Sonoran Desert their home.

WATER, WATER

Water is the limiting factor for the survival of living things in the desert. When humans interfere with the desert's delicate system of water distribution, disaster can result for the natural world. One of the first and most damaging human manipulations of the desert was the damming of the rivers. The Colorado River, a source of water for so much of the desert, was dammed to provide flood control and hydroelectric power. Over time, the river has also become a vital source of water for the cities and farms of Southern California. Irrigation has transformed the desert, turning large areas into orchards and fields of thirsty crops such as cotton. So many demands are made on the Colorado River that in dry years its once abundant

flow is reduced to a trickle by the time it crosses the border into Mexico. In the Colorado River Delta, a variety of habitats once flourished, ranging from saltgrass flats to freshwater ponds, from riverside forests to mesquite woods. Now little survives except for the very salty wetlands called the Cienega de Santa Clara.

People have also pumped water from the underground water table much faster than nature can replenish it. As a result, the level of the water table keeps dropping. This threatens the survival of the cities and towns that have come to depend on it, as well as the desert around the cities. Despite the scarcity of water, residents of cities such as Phoenix try to defy nature by planting lawns and water-hungry trees such as the ones they grew up with in the eastern United States, where water is more abundant. As the cities' demand for water grows, the price of water keeps increasing, putting many farmers out of business. Arizona is now home to many abandoned orchards and farms.

While water is usually scarce, the summer monsoon storms sometimes bring torrents. The torrents can cause flash floods, which threaten human property and life. To try to control the floods, governments have straightened out natural arroyos and washes and lined them with concrete to localize their flow. During a storm, rainwater rushes along the concrete ditches without soaking into and nourishing the surrounding land. Because its flow isn't diminished by vegetation or by twists and turns, and because the

> **THE RAPID GROWTH OF THE HUMAN POPULATION IS ONE OF THE GREATEST THREATS TO THE SONORAN DESERT.**

channels are straight and narrow, the water causes damaging erosion when it emerges from its concrete prison and tumbles into the arroyos and washes outside the cities. Water that flows through the city is also contaminated by a variety of pollutants such as engine oil and lawn fertilizer.

Fortunately, in recent years engineers have begun to realize that concrete channels are not a solution. Governments are prohibiting construction on desert floodplains and are turning natural washes into urban parks and pathways that preserve the natural environment while giving pleasure to the people that live around them.

CITIES IN THE DESERT

The rapid growth of the human population is one of the greatest threats to the Sonoran Desert. Once, the desert's stifling summer heat presented an unappealing environment for people. But modern air-conditioning systems for buildings and cars have triumphed over nature. They provide comfortable, protected environments for people year-round. In 1940, Tucson, the

MORE THAN 2,500,000 PEOPLE LIVE IN PHOENIX, ARIZONA.

second largest city in Arizona, had only 40,000 inhabitants. The 2000 census pegged the figure at almost 487,000. More than 843,000 people live in the metropolitan area surrounding Tucson. Metropolitan Phoenix is home to more than 2,500,000 people. Hermosillo, the largest Mexican city in the Sonoran Desert region, has more than 800,000 people.

Once, people moved to Arizona to escape allergies to the pollen of trees and other plants. Those same plants, however, have followed in the wake of the people who want to recreate familiar environments, and allergies are a problem there just as anywhere else.

Even when people decide to landscape their yards with native plants they can create problems for nature. Digging up wild saguaros is illegal, and nurseries now grow them from seed to sell as landscape plants. Saguaros grow very slowly, however, so big ones are sometimes dug up illegally and sold to homeowners. A big saguaro can sell for thousands of dollars, so the temptation to dig them up is great.

BIODIVERSITY IN DANGER

Recent human intrusions into the Sonoran Desert have affected the abundance of many species much more than the changes brought by early peoples. Ninety percent of the cottonwoods that once lined the banks of Sonoran Desert rivers

NURSERIES IN DESERT CITIES AND TOWNS SELL CACTI FOR HOME GARDENS.

have disappeared, victims of damming, agriculture, and city building.

Species that once roamed the area, including Mexican wolves and black bears, are no longer present, even though they survive elsewhere. And the abundance of many species has declined as their habitat has been destroyed, leaving them vulnerable to the effects of local disasters such as flood or fire. As far as scientists can determine, however, so far only one species has become extinct because of the changes wrought by people: a little creature called Merriam's mesquite mouse.

The total area inhabited by native Sonoran Desert plants has been drastically reduced. Up to 60 percent of what was once the Sonoran Desert ecosystem is now inhabited by about 380 species of nonnative plants introduced by humans. Two African grasses have been brought in for different purposes. Buffelgrass was planted as livestock food, and more than 1,000,000 acres (400,000 hectares) of the Sonoran Desert ecosystem were destroyed. Lehmann lovegrass was

brought in by the federal government's Soil Conservation Service to control erosion. In Arizona, this species now covers more than 400,000 acres (over 160,000 hectares).

Adaptable alien species, such as tamarisk trees and aggressive Africanized bees, are pushing out native plants and animals at an alarming rate. But the fragmentation of the desert caused by the ever-increasing human habitation is considered the biggest threat to Sonoran biodiversity. When habitat is broken up into disconnected pieces, biodiversity suffers. For example, some animals need large areas in which to forage or to find mates. When their habitat is interspersed with orchards and cotton fields, freeways and malls, they can't get from one piece to another. Their food supply is reduced, and they may not be able to find a mate.

CONSERVING THE DESERT

Fortunately, many individuals and organizations are working to save the Sonoran Desert. The Sonoran Desert

Museum just outside Tucson works to educate people about preserving the desert. It helps coordinate volunteers who clear weeds from the Tucson mountain area and encourages people to plant native desert plants by letting them know which plants work best in home gardens. The museum helps coordinate the breeding and reintroduction of the Mexican wolf into the desert and has active public education programs for both adults and children.

The Coalition for Sonoran Desert Protection helps more than forty conservation and citizen groups work together to preserve the desert. They are using the Sonoran Desert Conservation Plan developed by Pima County (the Tucson area) and the U.S. Fish and Wildlife Service to gain the best protection possible for Sonoran Desert species and habitat.

Large areas of the Sonoran Desert are protected as parks and preserves. The Saguaro National Park consists of two protected areas around Tucson, while Organ Pipe Cactus National Monument, along the Mexican border, preserves a large area of the desert that is home to the organ-pipe cactus. In addition, several national wildlife refuges are in the Sonoran Desert, and the Native Americans living on reservations in the area have helped preserve large areas and continue to promote desert preservation. With so many people and organizations determined to preserve this unique and beautiful ecosystem, the Sonoran Desert is likely to survive for a long time to come.

SAGUARO NATIONAL PARK, NEAR TUCSON, ARIZONA, IS A WONDERFUL PLACE TO SEE THE SONORAN DESERT.

WHAT YOU CAN DO

PROTECTING DESERT ECOSYSTEMS

Water is vital to the survival of all life on earth. The desert isn't the only place where water needs to be conserved. Wherever you live, preserving this most important natural resource is critical, and there are many ways you can help.

• If you have a yard, talk to your parents about returning some of the lawn to a natural unmowed and unwatered state. This is especially important if you live in the western United States, where water is often scarce or available only in certain seasons. You will save on water as well as reduce pollution and save on energy by reducing mowing. In many areas, you can buy seeds for native grasses and wildflowers. Be sure to check local regulations, since mowed lawns are required in some areas.

• If you live in the western United States, find out if desert wildlife refuges, parks, and preserves exist in your area. If you belong to a scout troop or other youth club, organize your group to volunteer. Preserves and refuges can always use people to help pull out nonnative plants and perform other chores.

• Learn more about deserts and give an oral report in your classroom about the subject so your fellow students can come to appreciate this special type of ecosystem.

WHAT HAPPENS IN THE FUTURE? YOU CAN BE INVOLVED

Keep up on proposals on the national level that will affect our deserts and write to the president and your congressional representatives. Here are some addresses you can use.

To write to the President:
The President
The White House
Washington, DC 20500

To write to the senators from your state:

The Honorable (name of your senator)
United States Senate
Washington, DC 20510

To write to your representative in Congress:

The Honorable (name of your representative)
U.S. House of Representatives
Washington, DC 20515

WEBSITES TO VISIT FOR MORE INFORMATION

There are many websites with more information about the Sonoran Desert and other deserts in North America. Here are a few of the most useful ones:

Arizona-Sonora Desert Museum

<http://www.desertmuseum.org>
The Arizona-Sonora Desert Museum in Tucson, Arizona, is a beautiful, mostly outdoor living museum of the desert. Its website has lots of interesting information about the Sonoran Desert, as well as information about their many educational and conservation programs.

Desert USA

<http://www.desertusa.com>
This site has information about all the different types of American deserts, including fact sheets on many of the plants and animals that live there.

The International Sonoran Desert Alliance

<http://www.charityadvantage.com/isda/HOME.asp>
The alliance's goal is to encourage a healthy, positive relationship between the Sonoran Desert, its inhabitants, and the needs of humanity. Its website has links to other organizations, information about protected lands, and other helpful websites.

Protect the Sonoran Desert

<http://www.sonorandesert.org/>
This is the website of the Coalition for Sonoran Desert Protection, an organization that strives to help preserve the Sonoran desert. Visit their website to find out how you can help.

FOR FURTHER READING

Johnson, Rebecca L. *A Walk in the Desert.* Minneapolis: Carolrhoda Books, 2001.

McClung, Robert M. *Lost Wild America: The Story of Our Extinct and Vanishing Wildlife.* Hamden, CT: Linnet Books, 1993.

McMahon, James A. *Deserts.* New York: Knopf, 1985.

Olin, George. *House in the Sun: A Natural History of the Sonoran Desert.* Tucson: Southwest Parks and Monuments Association, 1994.

Patent, Dorothy Hinshaw. *Biodiversity.* New York: Clarion Books, 1996.

Phillips, Steven J., and Patricia Wentworth Comus, editors. *A Natural History of the Sonoran Desert.* Tucson: Arizona-Sonora Desert Museum Press, 2000.

Scott, Michael. *Ecology.* New York: Oxford University Press, 1995.

VanCleave, Janice. *Ecology for Every Kid: Easy Activities that Make Learning About Science Fun.* New York: John Wiley & Sons, 1996.

Whitman, Sylvia. *This Land Is Your Land: The American Conservation Movement.* Minneapolis: Lerner Publications Company, 1994.

GLOSSARY

alluvial fan: a fan-shaped area of soil and rock carried by rain through aarroyos and washes and deposited on the desert floor

annual: a plant that lives for only one year

areoles: special places on the stems and pads of cacti from which branches, flowers, and spines grow

arroyo: a gully in the desert that carries rainwater

bajada: the area of the desert above the plains, formed by sand and gravel deposited by rainwater washing over the land

biodiversity: the variety of living things in an ecosystem

cacti: a family of plants without leaves, specialized for life in dry places

chlorophyll: the green chemical in plants that traps the energy of the sun

decomposer: a living thing that breaks down dead plants and animals into simple nutrients that can be used again by plants

ecological niche: the place of an organism within its habitat, which includes where it lives, what it eats, and so forth

ecosystem: a particular community of living things interacting with each other and their nonliving environment

endemic species: a species found in only one area

family: in biological science, a group of closely related organisms

glochids: tiny spines found on certain kinds of cacti

habitat: the environment in which a living thing lives

keystone species: a species upon which an especially large number of other species in an ecosystem depend

metabolism: the chemical processes of life

niche: the role an organism plays in its particular environment

oasis: a fertile area surrounding a spring or pool in the desert

photosynthesis: the process by which green plants use sunlight, carbon dioxide, and water to make their own food

pollen: the male reproductive material of a flowering plant, usually yellow in color

pollinator: an animal such as a bee, butterfly, or hummingbird that transfers pollen from one flower to another

primary consumer: a living thing that eats plants

primary producer: a living thing, usually a green plant, that converts the energy of the sun into chemical energy

replete: a special, individual ant whose abdomen is swollen with stored water or nectar

secondary consumer: a living thing, usually an animal, that eats primary consumers or other secondary consumers. Secondary consumers are also called carnivores.

sky islands: mountains in the Sonoran Desert that are surrounded by desert on all sides and are home to a variety of different ecosystems

stomata: tiny openings in the leaves and stems of plants

wash: a gully in the desert that carries rainwater

INDEX

ABOUT THE AUTHOR

Dorothy Hinshaw Patent was born in Minnesota and spent most of her growing-up years in Marin County, California. She has a Ph.D. in zoology from the University of California. Dr. Patent is the author of over one hundred nonfiction books for children, including *Life in a Grassland* (NSTA/CBC Outstanding Science Trade Book), *Apple Trees, Wild Turkeys,* and *Horses,* published by Lerner Publications Company, and *Dogs: The Wolf Within, Horses,* and *Cattle,* published by Carolrhoda Books, Inc. She has also co-authored gardening books and a cookbook for adults. She has two married sons, a grandson, and a granddaughter. She lives in Missoula, Montana, with her husband, Greg.

ABOUT THE PHOTOGRAPHER

William Muñoz has worked as a nature photographer for over twenty years. You can see his pictures of animals and plants in many books for children. Some of these books are *Life in a Grassland* (NSTA/CBC Outstanding Science Trade Book), *Watchful Wolves, Ants, Apple Trees, Wild Turkeys,* and *Waiting Alligators,* published by Lerner Publications Company, and *Horses, Dogs: The Wolf Within,* and *Cattle,* published by Carolrhoda Books, Inc. William lives with his wife and son on Vancouver Island in British Columbia, Canada.

PHOTO ACKNOWLEDGEMENTS

All photographs © Bill Muñoz, except: © John Flannery/Visuals Unlimited, p. 8; © Maslowski/Visuals Unlimited, pp. 9, 24; © Dorothy Patent, pp. 11, 23 (right); © David Muench/CORBIS, pp. 14, 18; © Joe McDonald/Visuals Unlimited, pp. 15, 21 (right); © John Muñoz, p. 19; © Rob & Ann Simpson, pp. 21 (left), 39; © Doug Sokell/Visuals Unlimited, p. 26; © Glenn Oliver/Visuals Unlimited, p. 35; © Joe McDonald/CORBIS, p. 37, 42; © Gerald & Buff Corsi/Visuals Unlimited, pp. 40, 47; © Charles Melton/Visuals Unlimited, p. 41; © Rick & Nora Bowers, p. 46 (left); © Arthur Morris/Visuals Unlimited, p. 46 (right); © Jan Butchofsky-Houser/CORBIS, p. 58. Maps and illustrations on pp. 10, 52, 54 by Bill Hauser.